How Weather Works

by Patricia Armentrout

A Crabtree Seedlings Book

CRABTREE
Publishing Company
www.crabtreebooks.com

Table Of Contents

Weather

Some days are cloudy and cold.
Some days are sunny and warm.

Sometimes it rains or snows.
We call this **weather**.

Clouds

The air we breathe has water droplets in it.

Find Out More

The water droplets in the air are so small you cannot see them—unless you look up at the clouds.

Clouds form when warm air **rises** and then cools.

Clouds can be different
shapes and different colors.

8

Thin, white clouds high in the sky usually mean fair weather.

Thick, puffy clouds hang lower in the sky. They can mean weather changes are on the way.

Low, dark clouds bring rain.

Lightning happens when electricity moves between clouds, or between clouds and the ground.

Thunder is the loud, rumbling sound you hear after lightning strikes.

Wind

Wind is moving air.

Wind moves things, like clouds.

Find Out More

Moving clouds change the weather around the world.

Nice weather sometimes brings light winds.

Light winds feel good.
They keep us cool and
can be fun.

Strong winds can move in suddenly with a storm.

Hurricanes and **tornadoes** make the strongest winds on Earth.

tornado

They can damage buildings.

Weather and Seasons

We **divide** the year into four seasons:

spring

summer

autumn

winter

Each season has different weather.

Spring brings rain. Summer is the warmest season.

Fall weather is cool. It causes leaves to fall from trees.

Winter brings cold days and snow.

GLOSSARY

divide (duh-VIDE): To split into parts

hurricanes (HUR-uh-kanes): Strong rotating windstorms

lightning (LITE-ning): The flash of light when electricity moves between clouds or between a cloud and the ground

rises (RIZE-iz): Moves upward

thunder (THUN-dur): The loud rumbling sound that comes after a flash of lightning

tornadoes (tor-NAY-dohz): Strong, rotating, columns of air that begin as a dark, funnel-shaped cloud

weather (WETH-ur): The day-to-day conditions of the outside air

INDEX

School-to-Home Support for Caregivers and Teachers

This book helps children grow by letting them practice reading. Here are a few guiding questions to help the reader build his or her comprehension skills. Possible answers appear here in red.

Before Reading

- **What do I think this book is about?** *I think this book is about how weather works. I think this book is about sunshine and lightning.*

- **What do I want to learn about this topic?** *I want to learn why the weather changes every day. I want to learn where rain comes from.*

During Reading

- **I wonder why...** *I wonder why the air we breathe has water droplets in it. I wonder why there are so many different kinds of clouds.*

- **What have I learned so far?** *I have learned that thin, white clouds high in the sky usually mean fair weather. I have learned that low, dark clouds bring rain.*

After Reading

- **What details did I learn about this topic?** *I have learned that thunder is the loud, rumbling sound you hear after lightning strikes. I have learned that wind is moving air that can move clouds.*

- **Read the book again and look for the glossary words.** *I see the word **lightning** on page 12, and the word **hurricanes** on page 19. The other glossary words are found on page 23.*

Library and Archives Canada Cataloguing in Publication

Title: How weather works / by Patricia Armentrout.
Names: Armentrout, Patricia, 1960- author.
Description: Series statement: Science in my world: level 1 |
    "A Crabtree seedlings book". | Includes index.
Identifiers: Canadiana (print) 20210204427 |
    Canadiana (ebook) 20210204435 |
    ISBN 9781427160553 (hardcover) |
    ISBN 9781039600027 (softcover) |
    ISBN 9781039600096 (HTML) |
    ISBN 9781039600164 (EPUB) |
    ISBN 9781039600232 (read-along ebook)
Subjects: LCSH: Weather—Juvenile literature. | LCSH: Meteorology—
    Juvenile literature.
Classification: LCC QC981.3 .A76 2022 | DDC j551.6—dc23

Library of Congress Cataloging-in-Publication Data

Available at the Library of Congress

Crabtree Publishing Company

www.crabtreebooks.com   1–800–387–7650

Print book version produced jointly with Blue Door Education in 2022

Written by Patricia Armentrout

Print coordinator: Katherine Berti

Printed in the U.S.A./062021/CG20210401

Content produced and published by Blue Door Publishing LLC dba Blue Door Education, Melbourne Beach FL USA. Copyright Blue Door Publishing LLC. All rights reserved. No part of this book may be reproduced or utilized in any form or by any means, electronic or mechanical including photocopying, recording, or by any information storage and retrieval system without permission in writing from the publisher.

Photo credits: shutterstock.com. Cover - weather icons © Thomas Amby, cover photo © Dmytro Balkhovitin; Title: IgorZh. Page 4/5©GM Vosd, Olga Sapeino; Page 6/7 © Photoongraphy; Page 6/7 © Serg64; Page 8/9 © Austin's Legacy Images; Page 10/11 © Jaros, Piotr Tominicki; Page 12/13 © 2009 fotofriends; Page 14/15 © MilousSK; Page 16/17 © Felix Mizioznikov, Alena Ozerova; Page 18/19 © Oiotr Tominicki, Delmas Lehman, page 19 tornado damage © John Wollwerth; Page 20 © photobank.kiev.ua; Page 21 Miroslav Hlavko, Maresol; Page 22 © Floris Sloof, Lou99; All images from Shutterstock.com

Published in the United States
Crabtree Publishing
347 Fifth Ave.
Suite 1402-145
New York, NY 10016

Published in Canada
Crabtree Publishing
616 Welland Ave.
St. Catharines, Ontario
L2M 5V6